Lerner *SPORTS*

T0016450

GREATEST OF ALL TIME PLAYERS

G.O.A.T. FOOTBALL
WIDE RECEIVERS

Josh Anderson

Lerner Publications ◆ Minneapolis

SPORTS THRILLS
MEET
RESEARCH SKILLS

Lerner SPORTS

Free Database Trial: **lernersports.com**

Lerner Publications Company
An imprint of Lerner Publishing Group, Inc.
241 First Avenue North
Minneapolis, MN 55401 USA

For reading levels and more information, look up this title at www.lernerbooks.com.

Main body text set in Aptifer Sans LT Pro.
Typeface provided by Linotype AG.

Library of Congress Cataloging-in-Publication Data

Names: Anderson, Josh, author.
Title: G.O.A.T. football wide receivers / Josh Anderson.
Other titles: GOAT football wide receivers
Description: Minneapolis, MN : Lerner Publications, [2024]. | Series: Lerner sports. Greatest of all time players | Includes bibliographical references and index. | Audience: Ages 7–11 | Audience: Grades 4–6 | Summary: "Wide receivers are the flashiest, most athletic players in the NFL. Meet wide receivers from the past and present and compare their skills, stats, and biggest plays"— Provided by publisher.
Identifiers: LCCN 2023012964 (print) | LCCN 2023012965 (ebook) | ISBN 9798765610206 (library binding) | ISBN 9798765623602 (paperback) | ISBN 9798765614860 (epub)
Subjects: LCSH: Football players—United States—Biography—Juvenile literature. | Wide receivers (Football)—Juvenile literature. | BISAC: JUVENILE NONFICTION / Biography & Autobiography / Sports & Recreation
Classification: LCC GV939.A1 A53 2024 (print) | LCC GV939.A1 (ebook) | DDC 796.33092/2 [B]—dc23/eng/20230323

LC record available at https://lccn.loc.gov/2023012964
LC ebook record available at https://lccn.loc.gov/2023012965

Manufactured in the United States of America
1 – CG – 12/15/23

TABLE OF CONTENTS

BIG PLAY THREATS

The San Francisco 49ers had won their first game of the 1988 National Football League (NFL) season, but they were in real danger of losing their second. The previous three years had ended with losses in the playoffs. The team needed to start this season strong.

The 49ers trailed 17–13 with less than a minute left in their game against the New York Giants. Nearly 80 yards from the end zone, quarterback Joe Montana took the ball. He looked down the field.

FACTS AT A GLANCE

» **JERRY RICE** IS THE NFL'S ALL-TIME LEADER IN CATCHES, RECEIVING YARDS, AND RECEIVING TOUCHDOWNS.

» SEVERAL WIDE RECEIVERS HAVE WON THE SUPER BOWL MOST VALUABLE PLAYER (MVP) AWARD. THEY INCLUDE **COOPER KUPP**, WHO HELPED THE LOS ANGELES RAMS WIN THE BIG GAME IN 2022.

» **CALVIN JOHNSON** OF THE DETROIT LIONS HAD 1,964 RECEIVING YARDS IN 2012, THE MOST EVER IN A SINGLE SEASON.

» SOME OF THE BEST **WIDE RECEIVERS** OF ALL TIME WERE TEAMMATES. JERRY RICE AND TERRELL OWENS PLAYED TOGETHER FOR THE SAN FRANCISCO 49ERS. RANDY MOSS AND CRIS CARTER WERE WITH THE VIKINGS AT THE SAME TIME.

49ers wide receiver Jerry Rice was a step in front of his defender. Rice was the team's best player. Montana tossed a long pass his way. Rice caught the ball and raced all the way to the end zone. His 78-yard touchdown won the game for the 49ers. The win kept San Francisco on a path that would end with a Super Bowl victory at season's end.

When football began more than 100 years ago, the forward pass was not allowed. In 1933, a rule change gave teams more freedom to pass the ball. Over time, passing has become a much bigger part of the game. To have a great passing game, a team needs great wide receivers. They need to be fast to get away from defenders. The NFL's best receivers make amazing catches look easy.

Cooper Kupp (*right*) of the Los Angeles Rams catches the winning touchdown in the 2022 Super Bowl.

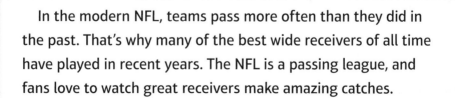

Wide receiver Reggie Wayne (*left*) and quarterback Peyton Manning (*right*) line up for the next play.

In the modern NFL, teams pass more often than they did in the past. That's why many of the best wide receivers of all time have played in recent years. The NFL is a passing league, and fans love to watch great receivers make amazing catches.

JUSTIN JEFFERSON

The Minnesota Vikings chose Justin Jefferson in the first round of the 2020 NFL Draft. He took the league by storm. In his first three seasons with the Vikings, he became one of the NFL's top wide receivers. After the 2022 season, he was the NFL's all-time leader with an average of 96.5 receiving yards per game.

Fans love Jefferson's well-known touchdown dance. Every time he scores, he does the Griddy in the end zone. Jefferson taps his heels while swinging his arms back and forth.

In 2022, Jefferson made a leaping, one-handed catch in the fourth quarter of a close game against the Buffalo Bills. Many fans considered it the best catch of the year. He finished 2022 with 1,809 receiving yards, the sixth-most in a single NFL season.

JUSTIN JEFFERSON STATS

Catches	324
Receiving Yards	4,825
Touchdown Catches	25
Pro Bowls	3

Stats are accurate through the 2022 NFL season.

CALVIN JOHNSON

Calvin Johnson was one of the biggest wide receivers of all time. He stood 6 feet 5 inches (2 m) and weighed 237 pounds (108 kg). His height and strength allowed him to outleap and outmuscle defenders. His size and power also earned him the nickname Megatron.

Johnson set an NFL record in 2012 when he finished the season with 1,964 receiving yards. He topped 1,000 receiving yards during seven of his nine NFL seasons.

Megatron had his greatest game ever in a 2013 contest against the Dallas Cowboys. He made 14 catches for 329 yards, the second-most ever gained in an NFL game. Johnson entered the Pro Football Hall of Fame in 2021.

CALVIN JOHNSON STATS

🏈	Catches	731
🏈	Receiving Yards	11,619
🏈	Touchdown Catches	83
🏈	Pro Bowls	6

CRIS CARTER

Hall of Famer Cris Carter was a master at scoring touchdowns. He always seemed to find open space in the end zone. And when the pass was near the sideline, Carter could reach out to catch it and keep his toes in the field of play.

During his 16 years as a pro, Carter led the NFL in touchdown catches three times. He finished his career with 130 touchdown catches, ranking fourth all-time. He also ranks 13th all-time with 13,899 receiving yards.

One key to Carter's long and successful NFL career was his ability to stay healthy. Carter was one of the toughest players of his time. He played in every game for 13 of his 16 seasons.

From 1998 to 2001, Carter and wide receiver Randy Moss were teammates on the Minnesota Vikings. Together, they formed one of the greatest receiver pairs of all time.

CRIS CARTER STATS

Catches	1,101
Receiving Yards	13,899
Touchdown Catches	130
Pro Bowls	8

Marvin Harrison spent his entire 13-year NFL career with the Indianapolis Colts. During that time, Harrison was part of one of the most fearsome offenses in NFL history. With Harrison, the Colts finished in the top four in scoring eight times.

Harrison's 1,102 catches rank fifth in NFL history. He also ranks fifth in touchdown catches with 128. His 143 catches in 2002 are the third-most ever in an NFL season. During his career, he led the NFL in catches twice, receiving yards twice, and touchdown catches once.

Harrison was a key player in the Colts' 2007 Super Bowl win. He finished the 29–17 victory over the Chicago Bears with five catches for 59 yards. Harrison is a member of the Pro Football Hall of Fame.

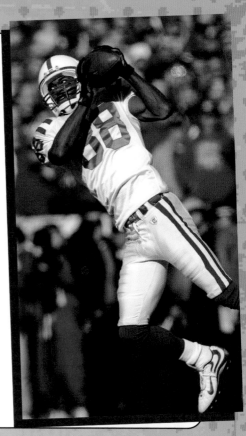

MARVIN HARRISON STATS

Catches	1,102
Receiving Yards	14,580
Touchdown Catches	128
Pro Bowls	8

Lance Alworth played most of his career in the American Football League (AFL) before it joined with the NFL in 1970. Alworth was one of the AFL's brightest stars. He played for the San Diego Chargers.

Before turning pro, Alworth was a football and track-and-field star at the University of Arkansas. A teammate gave him the nickname Bambi. The teammate said Alworth had a baby face and could run like a deer.

Alworth led the AFL three times in catches, receiving yards, and touchdown catches. He caught at least one pass in every game for an incredible 105 games in a row.

Alworth entered the Pro Football Hall of Fame in 1978. He was included on the NFL's 100th Anniversary All-Time Team. Alworth is also a member of the Hall of Fame's All-Time AFL Team.

LANCE ALWORTH STATS

🏈	Catches	542
🏈	Receiving Yards	10,266
🏈	Touchdown Catches	85
🏈	Pro Bowls	7

TERRELL OWENS

From 1996 to 2010, Terrell Owens played for five different NFL teams. He spent eight seasons with the San Francisco 49ers, including five with wide receiver Jerry Rice as a teammate. The Rice-Owens pair is one of the best in NFL history.

Owens ranks third all-time with 15,934 receiving yards. He also ranks third all-time with 153 touchdown catches. His 1,078 catches are the eighth-most in NFL history. Owens is the only player in the NFL to have an 800-yard receiving season with five different teams. The Hall of Famer is also the only player to score a touchdown against all 32 NFL teams.

Owens was a larger-than-life player known for his wild celebrations. He once grabbed a fan's cup of popcorn and poured some into his own mouth after a catch. In a game against the Seattle Seahawks, he celebrated a touchdown by pulling a marker from his sock and signing the ball.

TERRELL OWENS STATS

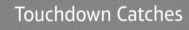 Catches	1,078
Receiving Yards	15,934
Touchdown Catches	153
Pro Bowls	6

LARRY FITZGERALD

To many football fans, Larry Fitzgerald is known as Larry Legend. He played 17 seasons, all with the Arizona Cardinals. Few players in NFL history can match his success on the field.

Fitzgerald ranks second all-time with 1,432 catches. His 17,492 career receiving yards also rank second in NFL history. His 121 touchdown catches are the sixth-most of all time.

Larry Legend only missed nine games in his entire career. Only Jerry Rice has played more than Fitzgerald's 263 career NFL games as a wide receiver. Fitzgerald twice led the league in touchdown catches. He also finished as the league leader in catches two times.

Fitzgerald helped Arizona reach the 2009 Super Bowl, where they lost to the Pittsburgh Steelers. He finished the 2009 playoffs and Super Bowl with 546 yards and seven touchdowns. Both are the most ever in a single NFL postseason.

LARRY FITZGERALD STATS

🏈 Catches	1,432
🏈 Receiving Yards	17,492
🏈 Touchdown Catches	121
🏈 Pro Bowls	11

DON HUTSON

Don Hutson played for a Green Bay Packers team that used the forward pass more than most other teams did at the time. He played more like a modern wide receiver than other pass catchers in the league. Hutson was one of the first to run many of the routes that wide receivers still use.

Hutson led the NFL in receiving touchdowns nine times and receiving yards seven times. It was not unusual to play both offense and defense in the 1930s and 1940s. In 1940, Hutson led the NFL in interceptions. He also served as Green Bay's kicker.

In the NFL's early years, Hutson was part of one of the league's great teams. Under Packers founder and head coach Curly Lambeau, Hutson helped lead the Packers to three NFL Championships. The NFL Championship was the league's top prize before the first Super Bowl in 1967. Hutson became part of the Pro Football Hall of Fame in 1963.

DON HUTSON STATS

Catches	488
Receiving Yards	7,991
Touchdown Catches	99
Pro Bowls	4

RANDY MOSS

Standing 6 feet 4 inches (1.9 m), Randy Moss was tall, fast, and skilled. He used his great speed and jumping ability to make catches when he was surrounded by defenders. Moss played for five teams in 14 years, including eight seasons with the Minnesota Vikings.

Moss ranks second all-time in the NFL with 156 touchdown catches. His 15,292 receiving yards are the fourth-most of all time. He led the NFL in touchdown catches five times.

In 2007, Moss set the NFL's single-season record with 23 touchdown catches. He helped lead the New England Patriots to a perfect 16–0 regular season record. Moss scored a touchdown in the Super Bowl, but New England fell to the New York Giants.

Moss entered the Pro Football Hall of Fame in 2018. He was a member of the NFL's 100th Anniversary All-Time Team. No other wide receiver had Moss's size, speed, and ability to catch the ball.

RANDY MOSS STATS

Catches		982
Receiving Yards		15,292
Touchdown Catches		156
Pro Bowls		6

JERRY RICE

In 2010, the NFL ranked its top 100 players of all time. Only two wide receivers made the top 30. Don Hutson came in at number nine, and Jerry Rice was number one.

  Rice's stats begin to tell the story of his greatness. His 1,549 catches, 22,895 receiving yards, and 197 touchdown catches all rank first in NFL history. He led the league in receiving yards six times, finishing with more than 1,000 yards an incredible 14 times. He also led the league in touchdown catches six times. His 20 seasons in the league are the most of any wide receiver.

But it was Rice's ability to lead his teams to victory that made him a true NFL legend and a Hall of Famer. He played 16 seasons for the San Francisco 49ers. The team made the playoffs 13 times and won three Super Bowls with Rice on the field. He was at his best in big games. Rice scored 22 touchdowns in the postseason, including eight in the Super Bowl. The greatest wide receiver of all time always stepped up when his teams needed him the most.

JERRY RICE STATS

🏈	Catches	1,549
🏈	Receiving Yards	22,895
🏈	Touchdown Catches	197
🏈	Pro Bowls	13

EVEN MORE G.O.A.T.

There have been so many amazing wide receivers throughout football history. Choosing only 10 is a challenge. Here are 10 others who could have made the G.O.A.T. list.

....

No. 11	STEVE LARGENT
No. 12	RAYMOND BERRY
No. 13	TIM BROWN
No. 14	ELROY HIRSCH
No. 15	PAUL WARFIELD
No. 16	REGGIE WAYNE
No. 17	JULIO JONES
No. 18	ISAAC BRUCE
No. 19	STEVE SMITH SR.
No. 20	COOPER KUPP

YOUR G.O.A.T.

It's your turn to make a wide receiver G.O.A.T. list. If some of your favorite players don't play wide receiver, make a list for another position too! You can also make G.O.A.T. lists for movies, books, and other things you like.

Start by doing research. You can check out the Learn More section on page 31. The books and websites listed there will help you learn more about football players of the past and present. You can also search online for even more information about great players.

Once you have your list, ask friends and family to create their lists. Compare them and see how they differ. Do your friends have different opinions about the greatest players? Talk it over and decide whose G.O.A.T. list is your favorite.

GLOSSARY

defense: players on a football team who try to keep the other team from scoring

end zone: the area at each end of a football field where players score touchdowns

founder: a person who takes the first steps to build something new

Hall of Famer: a retired player who is honored in the Pro Football Hall of Fame

interception: a pass caught by the defending team that results in a change of possession

NFL Draft: a yearly event when NFL teams take turns choosing new players

offense: players on a football team who try to score points

postseason: games played after the regular season to determine a champion

pro: short for *professional*, taking part in an activity to make money

Pro Bowl: the NFL's all-star game

route: a path a wide receiver runs during a play

LEARN MORE

Frederickson, Kevin. *Wide Receivers*. Mendota Heights, MN: North Star Editions, 2019.

Jerry Rice Official Site
https://www.jerryricefootball.com/

Levit, Joe. *Football's G.O.A.T.: Jim Brown, Tom Brady, and More*. Minneapolis: Lerner Publications, 2019.

Mitchell, Bo. *Justin Jefferson*. Mendota Heights, MN: North Star Editions, 2023.

NFL 100th Anniversary Team: Official All-Time Roster
www.nfl.com/100/all-time-team/roster

Pro Football Hall of Fame
https://www.profootballhof.com/

INDEX

PHOTO ACKNOWLEDGMENTS

Image credits: Bettmann/Contributor/Getty Images, p.4; Focus On Sport/Contributor/Getty Images, p.5; Gregory Shamus/Staff/Getty Images, p.6; Andy Lyons/Staff/Getty Images, p.7; Stephen Maturen/Contributor/Getty Images, p.8; David Berding/Stringer/Getty Images, p.9; Jared Wickerham/Stringer/Getty Images, p.10; Focus On Sport/Contributor/Getty Images, p.11; Joseph Patronite/Contributor/Getty Images, p.12; Allen Kee/Contributor/Getty Images, p.13; Al Messerschmidt/Staff/Getty Images, p.14; Brian Bahr/Staff/Getty Images, p.15; Focus On Sport/Contributor/Getty Images, p.16; Focus On Sport/Contributor/Getty Images, p.17; The Sporting News/Contributor/Getty Images, p.18; Owen C. Shaw/Contributor/Getty Images, p.19; Norm Hall/Stringer/Getty Images, p.20; Otto Greule Jr/Stringer/Getty Images, p.21; Bruce Bennett/Contributor/Getty Images, p.22; Bettmann/Contributor/Getty Images, 23; Focus On Sport/Contributor/Getty Images, p.24; CRAIG LASSIG/Stringer/Getty Images, p.25; JOHN G. MABANGLO/Stringer/Getty Images, p.26; Brian Bahr/Staff/Getty Images, p.27

Cover: Focus On Sport/Contributor/Getty Images; DeFodi Images/Contributor/Getty Images, On Sport/Contributor/Getty Images